Comets

By Cameron Macintosh

Have you ever seen a bright object flying across the night sky? You might have seen a comet!

A comet is a frozen ball of dust, rock and gas that flies through space.

Comets have two “tails”.

The first tail is blue and made of gas.
The second one is yellow and made of dust.

As a comet gets closer to the Sun, its tails extend.
This means that they get longer.

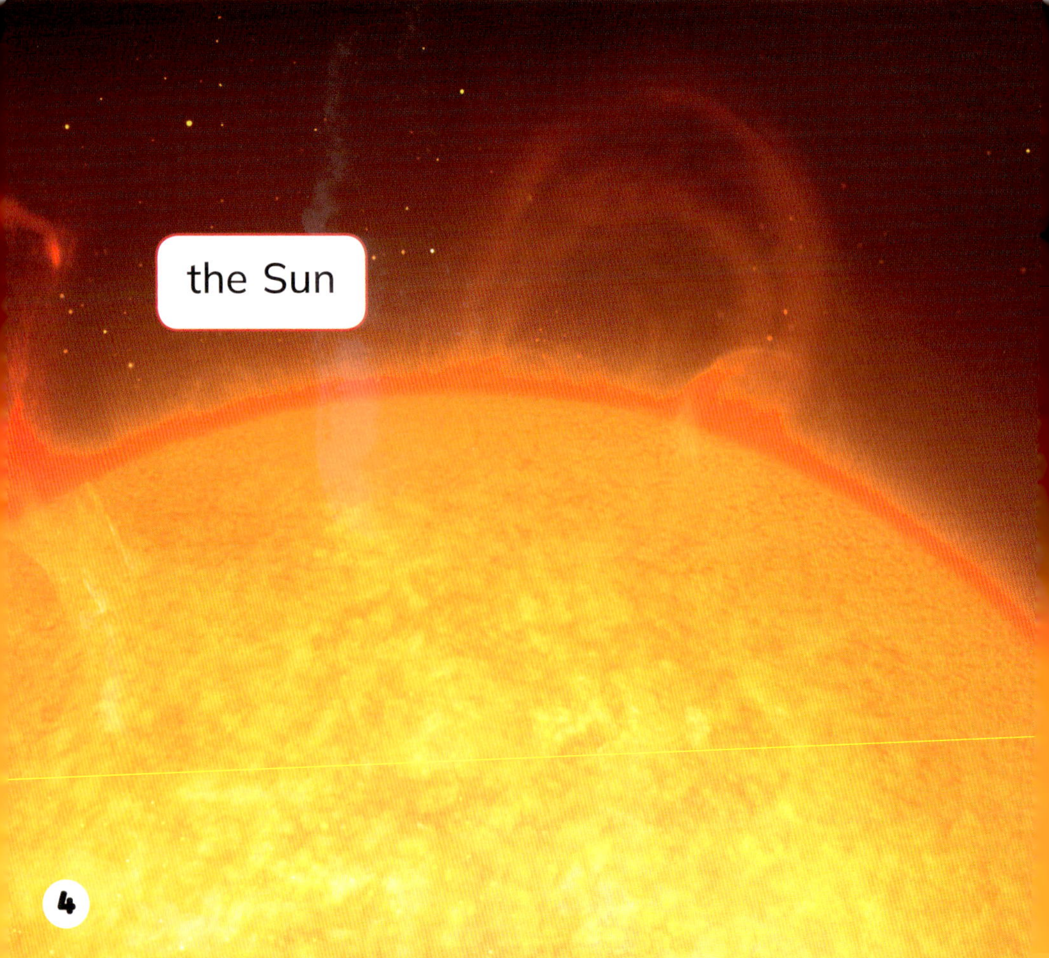

Comets can be huge.

The frozen rock plus the dust and gases can make some comets bigger than a planet!

Lots and lots of comets travel around the Sun.

Some comets even crash into the Sun!

Most comets do not get close to Earth.

It has been many, **many** years since a comet has hit our planet.

If a large comet hits Earth,
it makes a huge crater.

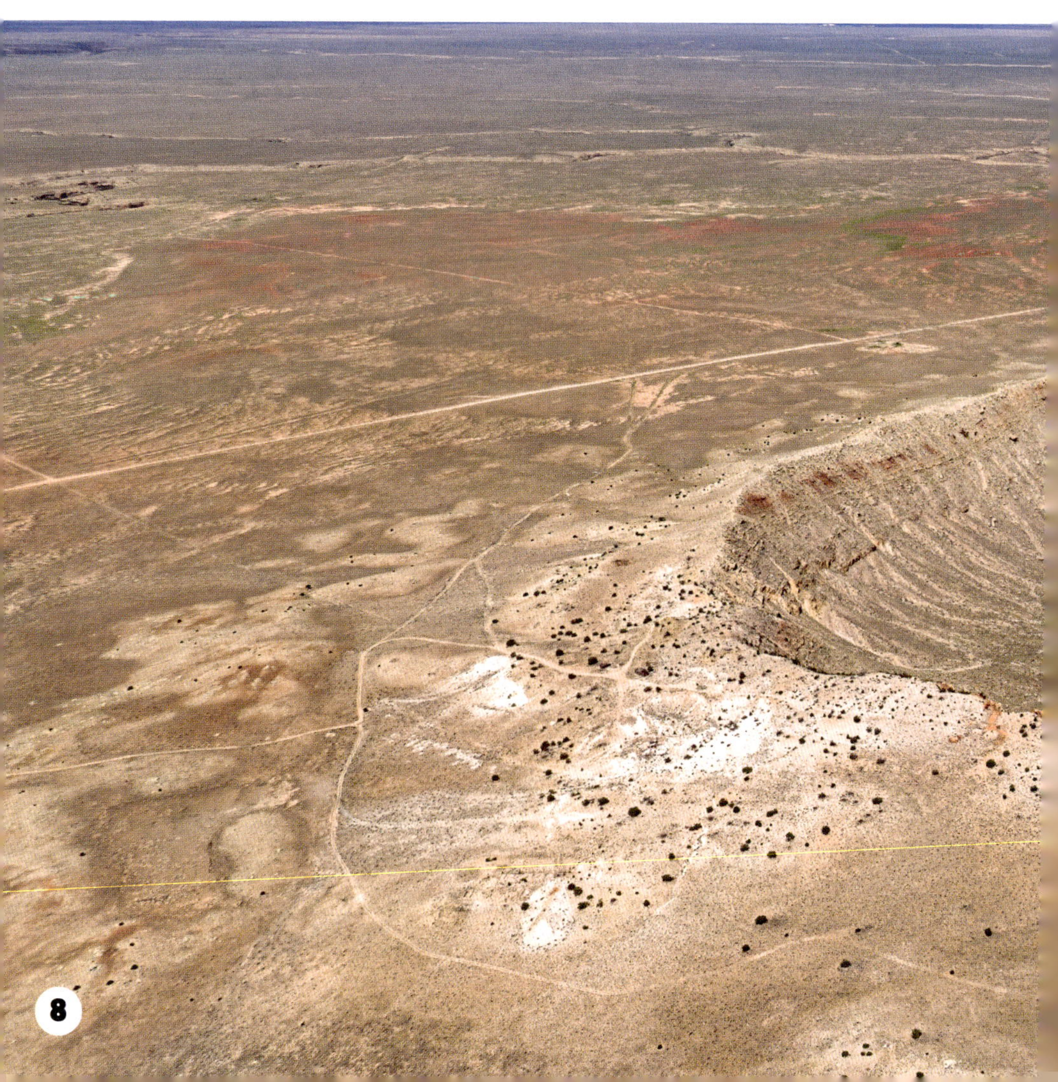

This crater was made almost 50,000 years ago in the USA.

People can locate comets by watching space.

They collect data on their laptops and use the data to track comets.

You can see a comet called Halley's comet from Earth – but not often!
It flies past our planet every eight decades.
Its most recent visit was in 1986.

Halley's comet in 1986

If a comet flies close to Earth, go outside after sunset to see it.

You will have to wait many years to see Halley's comet!

You can pretend the comet is a shooting star.
Take a moment to make a wish!

CHECKING FOR MEANING

1. What are a comet's two tails made of? *(Literal)*
2. How often does Halley's comet fly past Earth? *(Literal)*
3. Why do you think night-time is a good time to see comets? *(Inferential)*
4. If you made a wish on a comet, do you think it would come true? Why? *(Evaluative)*

EXTENDING VOCABULARY

frozen	How many syllables are in the word *frozen*? How many sounds are there? What is the base of the word *frozen*?
planet	What is a planet? What planet do we live on? What other planets are in our solar system?
locate	What does the word *locate* mean? How is the word *locate* related to the word *location*? What is another word the author could have used instead of *locate*?

MOVING BEYOND THE TEXT

1. How would you describe a comet?
2. What are some other things that you can see in space?
3. Would you like to go into space? Why?
4. What wish would you make if you saw a comet? Why?

TIME TO WRITE

Imagine you are going on a journey into space. What will you see? What will you do?